Your FINANCIAL BREAKTHROUGH

The ABCs of Turning Your Financial Crisis Into Your Financial Breakthrough

Dr. Cora L. Green

First printing 2021

ISBN: 978-0-9895443-2-0

This book is dedicated to you.
I pray that as you read on,
each chapter will inspire you
to begin the journey to
YOUR FINANCIAL BREAKTHROUGH.

This book is also dedicated to
my loving husband,
Ervin C. Green, who encouraged
and supported my endeavors.
He is the wind beneath my wings.

Last but not least, I also
dedicate this book to my children:
Phillipa Vernon,
George Vernon, and
Georgia Vernon.

Acknowledgments

Above all, I give the highest praise and thanks to God. Without Him, I would be like a ship without a sail!

Sincere thanks to Pastors Carl and Alice Stephens, Senior Pastors of Faith Assembly of God, for allowing me to use my gifting of "Teaching" to educate others and glorify God.

Gratitude goes to Dr. Faith Fredrick and Dr. David Bush at Faith Christian University (FCU). Upon obtaining my Doctoral Degree in Theology from FCU, they allowed me to create and implement Biblical Finance lesson plans and instruct students on being faithful stewards of God's finances.

Much appreciation goes to Rev. Dr. Oliver Phillips for his guidance, comments, and suggestions. If I had a question about this work, Pastor Oliver had an answer.

Special thanks to my nephew, Daniel Middleton, Jr., for his suggestions and instructions conducive to completing this work. As Creative Director of Scribe Freelance, he applied his innate expertise to this book's design, from cover to cover.

I acknowledge my children Phillipa Vernon, George Vernon, and Georgia Vernon.

I thank my sisters Bernice Craig, Patsy Middleton, and Rita Townes for their encouragement.

I extend sincere gratitude to my friends and colleagues, not mentioned, who contributed to this book's success. I could not have made it without your support.

Most importantly, I owe debts of love to my caring, loving, and supportive husband, Ervin C. Green, for his vital support, patience, understanding, and tolerance during the times I hibernated while writing this book. My heartfelt thanks to you for your willingness to manage our household activities while I completed this work.

Contents

Abstract

SPRING WAS IN THE AIR, and so was the Coronavirus disease of 2019. The contagion of this worldwide health pandemic was far-reaching and resulted in unprecedented sickness and death. The global economies were brought to a halt, attempting to stop the COVID-19 spread. The world, in an upheaval, was headed for a worldwide economic shutdown.

Like so many of the other nations, the United States of America was at war against COVID-19. In a desperate attempt to stop the spread of the disease, millions of Americans, at least 95 percent of families, were under stay-at-home orders.

These mandatory directives that prohibited individuals from going to work or school quickly swept across the Nation, and as a result, employment came to a screeching halt. More than 22 million unemployment applications flooded the Department of Economic Opportunity System in just a few weeks. The sudden overload caused the system to crash. While the system was undergoing an overhaul, the processing of the never-ending swell of application submissions was delayed and caused an income setback that, in turn, gave birth to a financial crisis.

Before the Coronavirus financial crisis, many individuals and families struggled to support their homes financially. Statistics suggest that, in the long run, due to COVID-19, about 50 million individuals could be affected by unemployment. A survey by Bankrate indicates that approximately 76 percent of individuals and families live paycheck-to-paycheck.[1] For individuals in this category, having more end of the month than money is normal.

Another study, also performed by Bankrate, indicates that most

1 Bankrate. Jan. 16, 2019

Americans do not have at least $1000 on hand in an emergency fund to weather the storm.[2] Life happens, and emergencies arise. Financial storms will come. They come in the form of "Time and Chance."

> *I returned and saw under the*
> *sun that the race is not to the*
> *swift, nor the battle to the strong,*
> *neither yet bread to the wise, nor*
> *yet riches to men of understanding,*
> *nor yet favor to men of skill, but time*
> *and chance happeneth to them all.*
>
> —*Ecclesiastes 9:11*

So, what are we supposed to do when we are in the midst of a financial crisis and need a breakthrough? We must trust in the Lord more than ever and lean not unto our understanding. Proverbs 3:5-6 says, "Trust in the LORD with all thine heart and lean not unto thine own understanding. In all thy ways acknowledge him, and he shall direct thy paths."

The world plunged into the COVID-19 health crisis described as the worse HEALTH crisis in more than 100 years, compounded by the worse FINANCIAL crisis in many years. Governmental authorities provided temporary financial relief for individuals, families, and businesses, but this was not enough to stimulate the economy. Before long, individuals and families everywhere needed a ***financial breakthrough***.

A BREAKTHROUGH FROM YOUR FINANCIAL CRISIS IS JUST AROUND THE CORNER

IT IS TIME TO RESET YOUR PERSONAL FINANCE BUTTONS!

A financial breakthrough is something almost everyone wants but getting one can be difficult if the right steps are not taken. Obtaining a financial

2 Ibid

breakthrough depends on your desire to effect change. No one else, but YOU will decide to move beyond whatever is your resistance to change.

You can do it! You can obtain your financial breakthrough! Remember, with God, all things are possible. (Matthew 19:26)You can do all things through Christ who strengthens you. (Philippians 4:13) God has not given you a spirit of fear but of power, love, and a sound mind. (2 Timothy 1:7) Therefore, do not procrastinate. Do not wait for a more convenient time. The time to start or to jump-start the pursuit of your financial breakthrough is now. READ ON! Be sure to follow every principle and detail discussed below and begin the journey to your financial breakthrough.

Could it be that you have been acting as the owner of the monies in your possession and managing according to your management styles, placing priorities in your order instead of God's order?

THE TIME FOR CHANGE IS NOW!

WHAT YOU ARE DOING WITH MONEY IS PRODUCING THE RESULTS YOU ARE GETTING!

Allow the true owner to show you how to rightfully manage, according to His principles, in order of His priorities, not yours. Only then can you prosper and be in health, even as your soul prospers (3 John 1:2), and live the life that God designed specifically for you from the foundations of the world. God offers you a life of meaning and purpose—a life wherein you are:

- The head, and not the tail; Above only and not beneath.
  Deuteronomy 28:13
- Lenders, not borrowers
  Proverbs 22:7
- Blessed coming in and blessed going out
  Deuteronomy 28:6
- Prosperous in everything you do
  Deuteronomy 29:9

Introduction

MONEY IS DEEPLY WOVEN INTO the fabric of our lives. It plays a significant role in each of our financial lives. We earn it, spend it, save it, and invest it. Many of us worry about it. We get sick from financial stress and end up having to spend more on medical bills.

Perhaps you are overwhelmed by the constant financial struggles you encounter. Having tried everything you know and not knowing what else to do, you built mental or emotional walls of protection around you. Your walls entrap your financial problems on the inside while at the same time, keep out those who can help you. Such walls quickly become barriers that block help from the outside. You feel like life is impossible, and you will never win with money. Your only hope is for a **breakthrough**!

Maybe you did not erect walls of protection but find that your money train has somehow derailed. You feel that you have tried everything you know to improve your financial situation, but success is nowhere in sight. Getting back on track seems impossible. You are about to throw in the towel. Like so many other individuals, you need a new way of looking at your situation. Your only hope is for a financial **breakthrough**!

According to thefreedictionary.com, the word "**breakthrough**" is defined as:

1. An act of overcoming or penetrating an obstacle or restriction.
2. A military offensive that penetrates an enemy's lines of defense.
3. A significant achievement or success that permits further progress, as in technology.

Harold Herring defines breakthrough as:

A sudden burst of revelation that enthusiastically moves you beyond all previous points of past resistance bringing you to a new level of success.

Herring goes on to say that "you...nobody else but you...will make a decision to move beyond the boundaries that societal inertia or attacks of the enemy have taken you."[3]

A person may experience a financial struggle or become financially derailed and need a financial breakthrough for several reasons. To name a few:

1. Generational Stronghold
2. Laziness / Slackness
3. Lack of Financial Literacy
4. Disobedience

Generational Stronghold: Ignorance and rebellion are symptoms of a generational stronghold. For example, after seeing their grandparent(s) and their parent(s) time after time displaying ignorance or disobedience to God's Word, children are usually inclined to believe that such behaviors are normal and acceptable, and they repeat the learned behaviors. The child's actions typically speak louder than words saying: "Grandma did it this way, Mama did it this way, and therefore, it is okay if I do it this way."

Parents should lead by example. They should demonstrate their obedience to God's financial principles and instill those behaviors within their children.

Train up a child in the way he should go and when he is old, he will not depart from it. (Proverbs 22:6)

All your children shall be taught of the Lord, and great shall be their peace. (Isaiah 54:13)

The cure for a generational stronghold is repentance, followed by obedience through faith in Christ and a life consecrated to God. (Romans 12:1-2) God saved Israel when they turned from idolatry to obedience.

3 Haroldherring.com

When they cried out to God, He raised up a deliverer for them. (Judges 3:9; I Samuel 12:10-11) God promises to show love to a thousand generations of those who love Him and keep His commandments. (Exodus 20:6) This Scripture proves that God's grace will last one thousand times longer than His wrath.

Laziness / Slackness: The word "sluggard" is used in the King James Version of the Bible. This term means the same as "laziness." To avoid being lazy or sluggish, we must be "...imitators of those who through faith and patience, inherited the promises." (Hebrews 6:12) The Bible says that if we are lazy or slack, we will experience poverty. Scripture admonishes us to work diligently at whatever our hands find to do.

> *He becomes poor who deals with a slack hand, but the hand of the diligent makes rich. (Prov. 10:4)*
>
> *The soul of the sluggard desires and has nothing; but the soul of the diligent will be made fat. (Prov. 13:4)*
>
> *How long will you sleep, O sluggard? When will you arise out of your sleep? Yet a little sleep, a little slumber, a little folding of the hands to sleep—so will your poverty come upon you like a stalker, and your need as an armed man. (Prov. 6:9–11)*
>
> *He also who is slothful in his work, is brother to him who is a great waster. (Prov. 18:9)*

We can become sluggards very quickly. The habit of slothfulness usually begins unnoticed. To overcome this habit, we must learn and apply discipline to our daily lives. Envision the size of the brain of an ant compared to the size of the brain of a human. The ant has:

> *...no guide, overseer, or ruler, (yet she) provideth her meat in the summer, and gathereth her food in the harvest. Proverbs 6:7–8*

Lack of Financial Literacy: You lack the skills, education, and understanding of various financial principles (such as giving, spending, saving, and investing) that would enable you to manage money wisely and effectively.

An article written by Iacurci, published in the InvestmentNews Periodical, dated March 2, 2019, refers to Financial Literacy as "An Epic Fail in America."[4] An Epic Fail is an embarrassing (financial) mistake that leads to a humbling situation. An individual in such a position is subject to ridicule. A person who lacks personal finance knowledge may make bad financial decisions that can subject them to be ridiculed by others.

Disobedience: Failure, refusal, or neglect to follow God's rules. Disobedience to God's Word demonstrates rebellion and mistrust. When we submit to God's Word and follow His Rules, we show acceptance of His will and authority over our lives. Our actions of obedience demonstrate our submission. What we believe is demonstrated by our behavior.

Jesus showed His love for His Father by submitting to His Father's will and being OBEDIENT, even unto death. Likewise, we need to show our appreciation for God by complying with His financial principles.

OBEDIENCE TO GOD'S WORD IS
A PERSONAL CHOICE!

DISOBEDIENCE TO GOD'S WORD BRINGS
DEATH TO OUR FINANCES!

Obedience is a choice that you MUST make if you are to win with money. God expects you to be obedient. Obedience to God's Word shows your love for God. Obedience ALWAYS brings blessings to you and others. For example, when you comply with God's financial principles, your entire family and others who are near and dear to you get to share in the benefits or rewards (blessings) that you receive in exchange for your obedience. When you are obedient to God's Word, you show that you trust Him in one of the most central areas of your life—finance.

When you exercise the FREE will that God has given you by choosing to disobey His commands, you are yielding to self-will instead of surrendering

4 Iacurci, Greg. InvestmentNews. March 2, 2019.

to God and desiring His will for your life.

A thorough assessment of the following four conditions ((1) ***a generational stronghold, (2) laziness / slackness, (3) lack of financial literacy, and (4) disobedience to God's principles)*** should reveal which one(s) is causing you to struggle. Once you become aware of the obstacle, you must immediately address the situation, change your course of action, become wholly obedient to God's Word, and begin to handle money God's way.

God wants to prosper you! He desires that you "...prosper and be in health, even as your soul prospers. (3 John 1:2) He wants to make you wealthy.

> *But you must remember the Lord your God, for it is He who gives you the ability to get wealth, so that He may establish His covenant which He swore to your fathers, as it is today. (Deuteronomy 8:18)*

When you are thriving financially, you show the world that God is a promise keeper. Decide today that you will begin to apply ALL of God's financial principles to your daily money management processes.

Now is the time!
Read on and step into your Season of Financial Breakthrough!

Chapter 1

THERE MUST BE A CHANGE OF HEART

IN THE PAST, I STRUGGLED to take control of my finances. After much effort and wasted years, I realized that I was not following God's financial principles. The bad choices I made, such as borrowing to satisfy my desire to obtain more stuff, combined with my love for instant gratification, caused my creditors to be in charge of my money.

As an accounting major, who should be able to account for my finances better than me? No one should. At least, that was what I thought. I had spent many years receiving a formal education in Finance and Accounting, and I certainly, clearly understood the concept of 2 + 3 = 5. Well, why did I find it so difficult to win at managing my money? I continued my financial quest for a financial breakthrough, and time after time, I repeatedly missed the mark.

Financial failures littered my life, one fiasco after another. The stream of economic defeats led to a financial breakdown. Absolutely nothing worked! During one of my never-ending financial pity parties, while I was broke, busted, and disgusted, I realized that I repeatedly tried to win with money by doing things my way instead of God's way. I adhered to my financial principles and agendas instead of God's. What a disaster! I was kicking against the "pricks."

In biblical times, an ox was used for plowing and threshing grain. An ox goad was a stick with a pointed piece of iron fastened to the tip. While the oxen were plowing the land, the farmers kept them headed in the right direction using the stick. The ox, by nature, is stubborn and strong-willed. At times, it would kick at the goads, and as a result, the pointed iron would pierce the animal's flesh. The more the animal rebelled, the more it suffered.

That was me! I created my financial philosophy. I decided how I would use **MY MONEY** (not God's money) that I earned to live the lifestyle I wanted to live. Sadly, the more I managed my finances according to my principles and philosophy, the deeper I sank into my financial quagmire of indebtedness.

Jesus was referring to the stubborn, goad-stick behavior when He said to Saul on the road to Damascus: "It is hard for you to kick against the pricks" (Acts 9:5; 16:24). I learned the hard way that doing things God's way, such as building my financial house upon God's foundational principles, was fail-proof. Before gaining an understanding of this lesson, I continued to kick against the pricks. The more I kicked and did things my way, the more I experienced one financial breakdown after another and suffered a succession of financial crises.

God's thoughts are different from ours. Unlike us, His emotions or feelings do not drive His thoughts. He is immutable (He cannot change). His principles also cannot change. They are timeless. They worked yesterday, they are working in our lives today, and they will continue to work forever.

> *For my thoughts are not your thoughts, Neither are your ways my ways, saith the Lord. For as the heavens are higher than the earth, so are my ways higher than your ways, and my thoughts than your thoughts. Isaiah 55:8–9*

When God solves mathematical equations, $2 + 3 \neq 5$ (2 + 3 may not equal 5). God can cause 2 + 3 to be = to any number He desires, the same as He fed 5,000 people with five loaves and two fishes, and there were 12 baskets left over after everyone had eaten. (Luke 9:16–18)

My case of financial mismanagement was not one of isolation. Instead, I was one person in a large group of others who, like me, encountered financial challenges and problems daily because of making bad financial choices. The truth is, regardless of whether individuals are high-, middle-, or low-income earners, many persons experience daily money challenges and struggle when it comes to managing their finances. Much like my past experiences, these individuals struggle because they have not accepted God's financial principles in their hearts. The first step to winning with finance is NOT crunching numbers.

IF WE ARE TO WIN WITH MONEY WE MUST FIRST ACCEPT GOD'S FINANCIAL PRINCIPLES IN OUR HEARTS

The first biblical ***financial*** principle given to us is "obedience." According to the Cambridge English Dictionary, "obedience is a basic idea or rule that explains or controls how something happens or works." In other words, obedience to God's financial principles explains or controls how we obtain financial breakthrough and can "...prosper and be in health even as our souls prosper." (3 John 1:2)

WHEN WE OBEY GOD WE POSITION OURSELVES TO RECEIVE HIS BLESSINGS

Throughout the Bible, we see God dealing with man, and in every occurrence, obedience is a requirement. The principle of obedience is NOT optional! God expects us to be obedient to His Word. God gave specific instructions to Adam and Eve in the Garden of Eden when He instituted the OBEDIENCE principle:

> *And the LORD God took the man, and put him into the garden of Eden to dress it and to keep it. And the LORD God commanded the man, saying, Of every tree of the garden thou mayest freely eat: But of the tree of the knowledge of good and evil, thou shalt not eat of it: for in the day that thou eatest thereof thou shalt surely die. Genesis 2:15–17*

Trying to obtain a financial breakthrough while being **disobedient** to God's principles is like trying to start your car in the morning when your battery was drained the night before because of some undetermined parasite that caused your vehicle to malfunction. Your battery is dead! You have only two options: jump-start the car or replace the battery. Whichever of these methods you choose, if you fail to get to the source and fix or remove the invasive parasite that caused the problem, the malfunction cycle will repeat itself, and the morning of day two will be a carbon copy of day one. Your battery will be dead again, and your engine will not start!

Your financial breakthrough works the same way. You need to get to the source or the root of your money problem and fix it. The source might be any one or a combination of the four reasons we listed as causes for financial struggles or financial derailment (generational stronghold, laziness / slackness, financial Illiteracy, and disobedience).

God is immutable. He is the same yesterday, and today, and forever. (Hebrews 13:8) His purpose for humanity has not, will not, and cannot change.

> *"Now, therefore, hearken, O Israel, unto the statutes and unto the judgments, which I teach you, for to do them, that ye may live, and go in and possess the land which the LORD God of your fathers giveth you. Ye shall not add unto the word which I command you, neither shall ye diminish ought from it, that ye may keep the commandments of the LORD your God which I command you."(Deuteronomy 4:1–2) KJV*

Obedience to God's Word carries great reward. God promised Israel that if they were obedient to His Word, they would live and go in and possess the land. One may think that from Israel's past experiences with God, they would have learned first-hand the importance of obedience to His Word. Nonetheless, time after time, they responded with rebellion and disobedience, the same as many of us do today. God instructed Moses to warn Israel that He would rain down judgment on them.

WHEN WE DISOBEY GOD'S WORD WE POSITION OURSELVES TO EXPERIENCE ALL KINDS OF POVERTY

Quite similar to His promises to Israel, God promises to bless us if we are obedient to His Word. In Psalm 19:10–14, the Psalmist, David, talks about a reward for our obedience to God's Word. This reward will be given to us, not in the future but here and now, as we live out our lives in this world.

> *No harm will overtake you. No disaster will come near your tent. For he will command His angels concerning you to guard you in*

> *all your ways; they will lift you up in their hands, so that you will not strike your foot against a stone.You will tread on the lion and the cobra; you will trample the great lion and the serpent. Because he loves me, says the LORD, I will rescue him; I will protect him, for he acknowledges my name. (Psalm 91:10–14) NIV*

The Apostle Paul tells us in I Corinthians 10:11, "...these things happened unto them for ensamples: and they are written for our admonition...." One would think that after reading the Bible stories that describe the consequences people in those days experienced because of disobedience to God's Word, we would be admonished to obedience and work out our salvation with fear and trembling. (Philippians 2:12) Nonetheless, we continuously fail to reflect on the stories in the Bible. As a result, like Israel, many of us end up living with the consequences of the wrong choices we made.

As can be seen, down through the ages, much has not changed regarding obedience to God's Word, and disobedience continues to persist among God's children. It seems that the modern-day Christian conveniently believes that because we are under the new covenant of grace, all that is necessary for fulfilling the terms of the covenant is that we love God and God's people.

God still requires obedience to His Word. He has not withheld instructions from us. When we rebel against God's financial principles, He admonishes us:

> *And why call ye me, Lord, Lord, and do not the things which I say? Whosoever cometh to me, and heareth my sayings, and doeth them, I will shew you to whom he is like: He is like a man which built an house, and digged deep, and laid the foundation on a rock: and when the flood arose, the stream beat vehemently upon that house, and could not shake it: for it was founded upon a rock. But he that heareth, and doeth not, is like a man that without a foundation built an house upon the earth; against which the stream did beat vehemently, and immediately it fell; and the ruin of that house was great. (Luke 6:46–49)*

Chapter 2

OBEDIENCE: THE KEY THAT OPENS DOORS

One of the first words a baby learns to say and understands is "no." When a parent instructs a child to clean up their room, whether or not they experience reactance depends on whether or not they believe they have the freedom not to do so. If an adult consistently made the child clean his or her room in times past, that child will experience no reactance. If the child was allowed to leave their room messy, they will feel like their freedom was invaded and, as a result, will be reluctant to clean the room.

It is quite common for teenagers to defy house-rules. Adults, likewise, are no exception to this rule. Most adults feel resentment when told what to do.

Science suggests that as humans, we all have an inner rebel. It is human nature not to want to be governed by someone else and told what to do. When we feel that someone else controls us and we are not allowed to think for ourselves, we believe our choices are limited. Often, our inner rebel rises, and we begin to ask questions or do precisely the opposite of what we are told to do. Such rebellious actions are referred to by Brehm as "Psychological Reactance."[5]

As free moral agents, we can choose how we live our lives and manage money. God wants us to obey His Word and apply His financial principles to our money management processes. The Holy Spirit can help you to overcome psychological reactance. **Obedience to God's Financial Principles is key to obtaining your financial breakthrough.** The

[5] Brehm, Sharon S. "Psychological Resistance: a Theory of Freedom and Control," Printed in the U.S.A., Nov. 14, 2013, p. 88.

proper handling of money becomes simple and easy once you understand where money comes from before learning how to manage it.

I grew up in a culture where money was never discussed at home. When it came to personal finance, silence was golden. In school, I learned the principles of Mathematics, but I cannot recall any lessons that pertained to money management. Thus, personal finance, the topic that has everything to do with managing money, was a mystery.

God never intended for His money management principles to be obscure, confusing, or impossible to understand. Obedience and application of God's financial principles lead to financial victory.

OBEDIENCE IS THE KEY THAT ALLOWS US TO LIVE THE ABUNDANT LIFE THAT GOD HAS PLANNED FOR US FROM THE FOUNDATIONS OF THE WORLD

For I know the plans I have for you, declares the LORD, plans to prosper you and not to harm you, plans to give you hope and a future. Jeremiah 29:11 NIV

Chapter 3

FOUNDATIONAL PRINCIPLES

NOW THAT YOU UNDERSTAND THE dire need for OBEDIENCE to God's financial principles let us examine the other three foundational principles that must be accepted in your hearts before you begin the practical application of creating your budget.

Having a solid foundation for your financial house is as essential as having a solid foundation for the physical home where you live. If you build a house without a solid foundation and then move in and take occupancy, you may be able to live comfortably for a short time before the sun, rain, wind, or snow weaken the earth and cause your structure to crumble.

The same principle applies to your financial house. It is only as strong as its foundation, and therefore, it needs to be built upon a strong foundation. Thus, it is of utmost importance that you apply the following four biblical financial principles to the foundation of your financial house:

1. Obedience
2. Creation
3. Ownership
4. Stewardship

OBEDIENCE is at the base of the foundational principles. All of the other financial principles rest upon these four principles.

THE PRINCIPLE OF CREATION

The Bible contains many scriptures that declare God as the creator of all things. For example, the Bible states:

1. In the beginning, God created the heavens and the earth. (Genesis 1:1)
2. The earth is the Lord's, and the fullness thereof; the world, and they that dwell therein." (Psalm 21:1) (The earth refers to the body of rock or soil on which we live, and the world relates to human existence—we are the world).
3. All things were made by Him; and without Him was not anything made that was made. (John 1:3)

These Scriptures clearly express that God is the source and owner of ALL things, including all the money. Nowhere is it recorded that God transferred ownership of His possessions to His people. According to these principles, individuals do not own anything. Everything belongs to God. However, God transferred stewardship of His properties to us. Therefore, all the material things that individuals claim they own rightfully belong to God. We are stewards or managers.

THE PRINCIPLE OF OWNERSHIP

As children of the Most High God, we are bought with a price. Our bodies are temples of the Holy Spirit. Therefore, everything we do must glorify God, including our handling of the finances He has placed in our care.

God instituted work in the first book of the Bible. God assigned a man to work as the caretaker of the earth and everything on the planet earth. Today, many individuals believe that they work to earn income and, therefore, own the monies they receive as a medium of exchange for their services rendered. They do not understand God's principle of provision, whereby He provides for them through their employers.

Our culture supports the idea that we own the material possessions God has placed in our care. Today, legal documents such as real estate deeds, automobile registrations, bank accounts, and investment certificates have our names on them. These legal instruments allow us to dispose of the properties described in the documents at will. Such control causes us to believe that we rightfully own the articles that are titled in our names, as described in the documents.

From time to time, many of us spontaneously repeat the American motto "In God We Trust," claiming to trust in God when, paradoxically, actions speak volumes and expressly display our trust in the material possessions we claim we own. Although the Bible forbids the glorification of anything or anyone other than God himself, many individuals glorify material possessions.

THE PRINCIPLE OF STEWARDSHIP

Stewardship is all-inclusive and encompasses everything you do. Stewardship surrounds your existence. A steward is an administrator who manages the affairs and possessions of his master and is fully accountable to his boss. Once you acknowledge that God owns everything and has given portions to you to manage, you must find out how He wants you to manage what He has given you. God never leaves anyone guessing. He is always specific. He expresses that He wants you to "faithfully" manage the things He has given you, according to His procedures as written in His principles. Many individuals ignore God's rules and manage their assets according to their philosophies.

A popular management style predominantly used by many is one wherein individuals pay themselves FIRST and pay everyone else, including God, after. The analogy is that if an individual pays others first, they may not have enough to pay themselves.

As good stewards, you cannot rely on the way things appear to be. You are required to faithfully obey the Word of God, follow biblical principles, and watch God take care of any financial shortages or other challenges you encounter.

Chapter 4

FINANCIAL LITERACY

Coupled with our carnal desires to disobey God's financial principles is our lack of "financial literacy." An article from *Investopedia* describes financial literacy as the education and understanding of various financial topics such as creating a budget, giving, saving, spending, and investing—topics related to managing our finances. Financial literacy education is rarely taught in our school system. The lack of financial knowledge, combined with the absence of the skills necessary to understand personal finance, can lead to poor financial decision-making. Such inadequacy can result in negative consequences. Often, in trying to fix the mess in their strength, many individuals fail and **miss the mark.**

Perhaps you are fed up with having more month than money. You are sick and tired of robbing Peter to pay Paul each month. Financial pressures brought on by unemployment, low to zero savings, unexpected bills, and bad decisions you made are destroying your financial house. As a result, you continue to encounter daily problems that, if not checked, could lead to financial ruin.

How much are you trusting God and standing on His promises to do what He says He will do? Why not trust in the Lord with all your heart and lean not unto your understanding? Why not acknowledge Him in all your ways, in everything you do, and allow Him to direct your path? (Proverbs 3:5–6)

God promises to:

1. Supply all your need according to His riches in glory by Christ Jesus. Philippians 4:19

2. Set thee on high above all the nations of the earth if you carefully keep ALL of His commands. Deuteronomy 28:1
3. Make you the head and not the tail. Deuteronomy 28:13
4. Blessings shall come on thee, and overtake thee if thou shalt hearken unto the voice of the LORD thy God. Deuteronomy 28:2

Are you trusting Him to make a way in areas of your finances where there seems to be no way? God has promised to do a new thing in your life—not tomorrow, not next month or next year, but right NOW!

> *Behold, I will do a new thing; now it shall spring forth; shall ye not know it? I will even make a way in the wilderness and rivers in the desert. Isaiah 43:19*

God has already made plans for your prosperity:

> *For I know the plans I have for you declares the LORD, "plans to prosper you and not to harm you plans to give you hope and a future. Jeremiah 29:11*

He has promised to open the floodgates and let financial prosperity flow.

> *I will open rivers in high places and fountains in the midst of the valleys: I will make the wilderness a pool of water, and the dry land springs of water. Isaiah 41:18*

God has given us many promises regarding His blessings in the Bible. Many of His blessings are unconditional, which means we do not have to do anything to receive them. When it comes to God's financial blessings, conditional terms of actions you must take precede each blessing.

Condition: But seek ye first the Kingdom of God, and His righteousness;
Blessing: All these things shall be added unto you. Matthew 6:33

Condition: Bring ye all the tithes into the storehouse and prove me now

Blessing: I will open the windows of heaven and pour you out a blessing, that there shall not be room enough to receive it. Malachi 3:10

Condition: Give and
Blessing: It shall be given unto you, good measure, pressed down, shaken together, and running over, so shall men give into your bosom. Matthew 6:38

Condition: Honor the Lord with your wealth and with the best part of everything you produce.
Blessing: Then he will fill your barns with grain, and your vats will overflow with good wine. Proverbs 3:9–10

Condition: Keep therefore, the words of this covenant, and do them
Blessing: that ye may prosper in all that ye do. Proverbs 3:9–10

Chapter 5

GETTING THROUGH TIME AND CHANCE

THE BIBLE REFERS TO UNFORESEEN setbacks, including financial challenges, as time and chance. According to the book of Ecclesiastes 9:11, "…time and chance happen to them all." You may experience challenging times, such as financial hardships. According to Luke 12: 6–7, God does not forget about the sparrow. You are more valuable than many sparrows. God will see you through difficult financial hardships. Nonetheless, His financial promises are conditional, which means, He expects you to do your part first, and then He will do His part.

Like any good father, God requires obedience. Disobedience will cause you to suffer the consequences of your choices. The book of Deuteronomy 28:15 states: "But if you disobey the Lord your God and do not faithfully keep all His commands and laws that I am giving you today, all these evil things will happen to you." One of the evil things could be financial problems.

Do not allow money problems to become an all-consuming, ever-present financial inferno in your life. The time to begin the journey towards your financial breakthrough is now! Do not wait for a more convenient time. Start with the first biblical financial principle, which is: "OBEDIENCE."

Partial obedience is disobedience, and disobedience is rebellion. When you choose to disobey God's financial principles, you deprive yourself of obtaining God's FULL financial blessings and hinder yourself from experiencing the breakthrough you so desperately need. The prophet Isaiah writes in 30:1—"Woe to the rebellious children says the LORD, who take counsel, but not of me; and who devise plans, but not of my Spirit, that they may add sin to sin."

Chapter 6

FINANCIAL STATEMENTS

What is Your Financial Condition?

KNOWING THE DETAILS OF YOUR FINANCIAL situation is one of the first things God requires on the journey to your financial-breakthrough. Ignorance of your financial status is NOT bliss. Not knowing the truth of where you stand financially should be of concern. In Proverbs 27:23, we read: "...know the state of your flocks and look well to your herds.

One mistake some individuals make is to try to use their memory to keep track of financial records. To succeed in personal finance, you must maintain financial records in electronic or paper formats.

It is common for individuals and families to owe more than they own and have a negative net worth without knowing it. If they took the time to create a Statement of Financial condition, they would have noticed that their finances were upside down. They would have been able to steer away from many of the financial pitfalls that obstructed their financial lives and detour to improve their future financial condition.

Before preparing a Statement of Financial Condition, first, list all your assets. Assets are things you own, such as houses, cars, and anything of value. Next, list all your liabilities. A liability is an existing debt or obligation—an amount owed to a creditor, such as a mortgage, car loan, credit card loan, etc. Making a list of your assets and liabilities is very helpful as the items will later be transferred to your Statement of Financial Condition. Your list of liabilities can also help you decipher the best order in which to pay off your debt, starting with the loan with the highest interest rate. Examples of assets and liabilities can be seen in Table 1 and Table 2 below.

In Bible times, a person's wealth was measured by the number of herds and the size of flocks that person owned. In today's societies, the analogy of herds and flocks is no longer common-place and has been replaced with the names of financial institutions such as banks. Whether God gives you herds, flocks, or dollars to manage, He requires that you—Know Our Financial Position. Such knowledge is acquired by creating a Statement of Financial Condition, also called a Balance Sheet.

The Statement of Financial Condition shows a snapshot of your Net Worth at a point in time. If you fail to create a Statement of Financial Condition, you will not get an accurate picture of your financial condition. Many refrain from creating this Statement because they believe their lifestyles do not warrant setting one up. In other words, they do not possess the items necessary to create such a document.

Others ignore creating a Statement of Financial Condition because they choose to continue to exist in a façade atmosphere. They remain financially tranquilized and repeatedly tell themselves that they are financially healthy, and their financial lives are okay. When the sedation wears off in later years, many are jolted into reality and, once wide awake, realize that they were drowning in debt all along. A Statement of Financial Condition (total assets MINUS total liabilities) can be seen in Table 3 below.

TABLE 1

LIST OF ASSETS

Checking	$75
Savings	100
IRA	3,000
Mobile Home	45,000
Honda	15,000
Total Assets	**$63,175**

TABLE 2

LIST OF LIABILITIES (DEBT)

(Liabilities)	Payoff Amount	Monthly Payments	Due Date	Interest Rate
Mortgage	$35,000	$750	1st	5%
Honda	13,500	400	10th	8%
Visa	4,000	100	8th	23%
Discover	3,500	80	12th	16%
Physicians	850	20	15th	7%

Total Liabilities: $56,850

TABLE 3

STATEMENT OF FINANCIAL CONDITION (INSERT DATE)

Assets		Liabilities	
Checking	$75	Mortgage	$35,000
Savings	100	Honda	13,500
IRA	3,000	VISA	4,000
Mobile Home	45,000	Discover	3,500
Honda	15,000	Physicians	850
		Total Liabilities	**$56,850**
		Net Worth (NW)	**$6,325**[6]
Total Assets	**$63,175**[7]	**Liabilities and NW**	**$63,175**[8]

PERCENTAGES FOR INCOME ALLOCATION

Creating your family budget is quite different from setting up your Statement of Financial Condition. To establish a successful budget, you will need to know how much income should be allocated to each category in your budget. Setting percentages of how much income goes to a particular expense is extremely important. This will help you see what adjustments you need to make to accomplish your financial goals, such as building an emergency fund, paying off debt, or saving for retirement. An excellent guide to follow is the "Recommended Percentage for Income Allocation"

6 Subtract your total liabilities from your total assets to get your net worth. Your total assets should be the same dollar amount as your total liabilities PLUS your net worth.

7 Both sides of a Statement of Financial Condition must always be in balance. Total assets MUST always equal total liabilities plus net worth

8 A Statement of Financial Condition is also called a balance sheet. Both sides of the balance sheet MUST always be in balance or equal to one another.

found in Dave Ramsey's "Financial Peace University Workbook." A copy of the Recommended Percentages Chart can be seen in TABLE 4 below.

TABLE 4

RECOMMENDED PERCENTAGES FOR INCOME ALLOCATION[9]

Number	Category	Recommended Percentage
1	Tithe/Charitable Gifts	10 – 15%
2	Savings	5 – 10%
3	Rent/Mortgage	25 – 35%
4	Utilities	5 – 10%
5	Food	5 – 15%
6	Transportation	10 – 15%
7	Clothing	2 – 3%
8	Medical/Health	5 – 10%
9	Personal	5 – 10%
10	Recreation	5 – 10%
11	Debt	5 – 10%

After completing your Statement of Financial Condition, you will be able to see whether you have a negative or positive net worth. A negative net worth is not the end of the world. Your net worth is a "measuring stick" that measures how well or poorly you manage money.

Your next step is to find out exactly where every dollar of your household income is going and check, using the percentages in TABLE 4 above, to see if you are spending more than you should in any area(s). Your goal is not to spend more than you have allocated to any category in one month. You must be aware of every dollar that comes in and goes out. The

9 Source: Data adapted from Dave Ramsey. *Financial Peace University Workbook.* (Brentwood, Tennessee: The Lampo Group, Inc., 2008), 52.

best way to do this is to create a Budget, also called a Spending Plan.

There MUST be a Plan!

FAILING TO PLAN IS PLANNING TO FAIL

Perhaps you never tried budgeting, or maybe you tried it, but it never worked, and therefore, you were never able to get on top of your finances. I encourage you to try budgeting. "God is able to make all grace abound toward you; that ye, always having all sufficiency in all things, may abound to every good work." (2 Corinthians 9:8)

Following are steps to create a budget. Begin by adding up all income from sources such as a paycheck, dividend, interest, pension, social security, rental income, bonus, gifts, child support/alimony, earned income credit, and tax refund to get your total income. A list of income can be seen in Table 5 below.

TABLE 5
INCOME
STEP 1: LIST ALL AVAILABLE INCOME

Salary/Wages	$2,000.00
Interest	10.00
Dividends	10.00
Rent (mobile home)	500.00
Other (alimony)	600.00
Total Income per Month	$3,120.00

Next, track your spending for one to three months. Tracking spending is essential. If you do not know how much you are spending on each category, you will not establish a plan that reflects your actual spending. Your tracking must be accurate. For example, if you allocate too much or too little in any area, your spending plan will not accurately mirror your cash flow. One way to track your spending is to review your bank transactions daily to capture the transactions that occurred each time you swiped your debit card. You may need to walk around with a notepad and pen to write down any cash transactions that will not show up in your bank transactions. After 30 to 90 days of tracking your spending, it is time to establish your monthly spending plan.[10]

Begin by listing the expenses you tracked. There are two types of expenses (Fixed and Variable).

Fixed expenses stay relatively the same each month. Most individuals will have the same items listed in their fixed expenses. Some everyday items found in most everyone's spending plans are rent/mortgage, electricity, gas, phone, food, and clothing.[11] A list of fixed expenses can be seen in Table 6 below.

TABLE 6

FIXED EXPENSE PLANNING
STEP 2A: LIST ALL FIXED EXPENSES
(FIXED EXPENSES DO NOT CHANGE OVER TIME.)

Tithe	$ 312.00 (10% of total income)
Mortgage/Rent	750.00 (from Table 2 above)
Retirement	100.00 (personal decision)
Automobiles	400.00 (from Table 2 above)
Insurance	50.00 (from Table 7 below)
Debt	200.00 (from Table 2 above)
Total Fixed Expenses:	**$ 1,812.00**

STEP 2B: LIST ALL PERIODIC FIXED EXPENSES

Many fixed expenses such as insurance and homeowner's association dues

10 "Build a Basic Budget: The Five-Step Spending Plan." Mountain American Credit Union. Online: https://www.macu.com/pdf/MEB_BasicBudget.pdf (31 March 2012).

11 See a list of fixed expenses in Table 6 below.

are not paid on a regular monthly basis but must be paid in full at a given time such, as quarterly, semiannually, or annually. These types of expenses are called periodic fixed expenses. If you do not plan for these expenses, they can become budget busters. Many individuals resort to using borrowed money from credit cards or personal loans to meet these obligations when they are due. If the funds are borrowed, the repayment amount creates a new line item in the spending plan, and, therefore, the spending plan needs to be revised. Depending on your budget's tightness, any additional expense may or may not fit into your income.

The spending plan must reflect the periodic fixed expenses. The monthly amounts must be calculated and set aside. To calculate how much you should allocate each month to meet these obligations when due, divide the annual payment amount by 12 (months in a year). The answer represents the amount that should be set aside in a savings account each month. Saving this amount each month will allow you to have the entire amount due in 3, 6, or 12 months.[12]

TABLE 7
PERIODIC FIXED EXPENSE PLANNING

Type of Expense	Annual Amount	Months	Monthly Amount
Insurance	600.00	÷ 12 =	50.00*

*Note: *Auto insurance is $600 annually. Divide by 12 to determine how much you should set aside each month to make the annual payment when due. Add the monthly amount to the fixed expenses in Table 6 above.*

After listing all fixed expenses, list all variable expenses. Variable costs change in proportion to usage. In other words, the cost of your electricity is determined by the units used—the more you use, the more you pay. A listing of variable expenses can be seen in Table 8 below.

12 See Table 7 below.

TABLE 8
VARIABLE EXPENSE
STEP 2C: LIST VARIABLE EXPENSES
(VARIABLE EXPENSES CHANGE FROM MONTH TO MONTH IN PROPORTION TO ACTIVITY.)

1. Food	$ 550.00
2. Utilities	250.00
• Electricity	150.00
• Gas	0.00
• Water	20.00
• Telephone	60.00
• Cable	20.00
Total Variable Expenses:	**$800.00**

Once you have tracked your total income (Table 1) and expenses (both fixed and variable) (Table 6 and Table 8), it is time to create your budget (Income minus Expense) (Table 9).

TABLE 9
INCOME MINUS EXPENSE

Total Income per Month	$3,120.00
Less: Tithe (10% of income)	312.00
Net (Spendable) Income	2,808.00
Less: Total Expenses	
Fixed: $ 1,812.00	
Variable: 800.00	2,612.00
Cash Available for Saving[13]	**$196.00**

13 Unallocated surplus is the money that is left over after all other obligations have been met. Put it in savings or spend it wisely.

THE 10-10-80 BUDGET PLAN

The 10-10-80 Budget Plan is highly recommended. Here is how it works. You give "First Fruits," 10 percent of your income to God (II Corinthians 9:27), after which you pay yourself 10 percent (Proverbs 6:6–8), and then use the remaining 80 percent to pay your expenses.

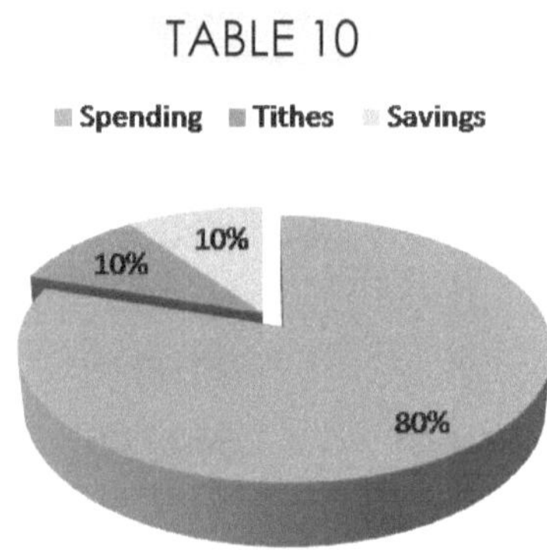

TABLE 11

MONTHLY SPENDING PLAN

	Amount	Total Amount
Income		
Salary/Wages	$0,000.00	
Interest	$0,000.00	
Dividends	$0,000.00	
Mortgage/Rent	$0,000.00	
Other	$0,000.00	
Total Income		$0,000.00
Fixed Expense		
Tithe	$0,000.00	
Mortgage/Rent	$0,000.00	
Automobiles	$0,000.00	
Insurance	$0,000.00	
Credit Cards	$0,000.00	
Total Fixed Expense		$0,000.00

MONTHLY SPENDING PLAN

Variable Expense		
Food	$000.00	
Utilities		
• Electricity	$000.00	
• Gas	$000.00	
• Water	$000.00	
• Telephone	$000.00	
• Cable	$000.00	
Total Variable Expense		$0,000.00
Total Expenses (Fixed & Variable)		$0,000.00

Income Minus Expense		
Total Income	$0,000.00	
Less: Tithe	$000.00	
Net (Spendable) Income		$0,000.00
Less: Total Expense		$0,000.00
TO or FROM Savings		$0,000.00

Chapter 7

STOP WRESTLING WITH GOD

You have victory over money. This triumph positions you to experience financial breakthrough over every adverse financial circumstance you encounter and allows you to continue to "Live in Financial Breakthrough." The Apostle Paul writes in I Corinthians 15:57: "But thanks *be* to God, who gives us the victory through our Lord Jesus Christ."Yet, many individuals continue to strive to win with money by their strength and continue to manage God's money using their financial principles, only to be defeated every time.

As you continue to struggle, you become more and more distracted from God and His Word. Interruption is a plan of the enemy. The thief comes to steal, kill, and destroy. (John 10:10) The enemy's job is to destroy you with financial problems that cause anxiety and fear and kill you with financial stress if you let him. This does not have to become a reality. "Greater is He that is in us than He that is in the world." (I John 4:4)

Many of God's children do not exercise victory over the enemy because they do not know who they are and whose they are, and as such, live beneath their privileges. They continue to disobey God's financial principles, encounter financial problems and wrestle with money, similar to Jacob's wrestling in Genesis 25–36.

> *And Jacob was left alone; and there wrestled a man with him until the breaking of the day. And when he saw that he prevailed not against him, he touched the hollow of his thigh; and the hollow of Jacob's thigh was out of joint, as he wrestled with him. And he said, Let me go, for the day breaketh. And he said, I will not let thee go, except thou bless me. Genesis 32:24–26*

GOD BLESSED JACOB BUT JACOB WALKED WITH A LIMP

Jacob's experience demonstrates that because your carnal minds cannot understand the things of the Spirit, you continue to wrestle with God for control over your finances, you remain in financial darkness. The Word of God is "...a lamp unto our feet and a light unto our path." (Psalm 119:105) Yet, so many of God's children disobey His Word and continue to fumble in financial darkness. While in the dark, you continue to make bad financial decisions and accumulate more bad debt. As your financial mess spirals out of control, you fight harder to control your finances in your strength. Realizing that you are not winning but instead are drowning in debt, you surrender and cry out to God in distress.

Throughout Scripture, from Genesis to Revelation, we read about individuals who were disobedient to God's Word. In each occurrence, we see the consequences of disobedience. In one example in Joshua 1:7, we read about how Achan disobeyed God's word and took items he was forbidden to take. Further along in chapter 2, verse 20, we see the result of his disobedience—the Lord's anger burned against Israel, and they suffered greatly. These lessons are written for our instructions. "For whatsoever things were written aforetime were written for our learning. (Romans 15:4) Also, I Corinthians 10:11 quotes: "Now these things happened unto them for ensamples: and they are written for our admonition, upon whom the ends of the world have come." We MUST Heed These Lessons.

RESTORATION

A "Financial Breakthrough" requires obedience to God's financial rules. Obedience brings healing and restoration from financial brokenness. Nonetheless, many individuals continue to drift away from God's principles and, therefore, wander away from Him. God is calling you. He wants to get you back on track.

> *Even from the days of your fathers ye are gone away from Mine ordinances, and have not kept them. Return to Me, and I will return unto you; saith the Lord of host. Malachi 3:7*

God wants you to choose to love Him and adhere to His principles. For this reason, He did not create you to be a robot. Instead, He created you with a free will to make choices. Sadly, your free will sometimes prompt you to go against God's original design for your life. Still yet, God loves you so much He wants to restore you to His original plan for your life wherein you can enjoy a life that is abundantly rich in every area, including finances.

> *Beloved, I pray that in all things thou mayest prosper and be in health, even as thy soul prospereth. 3 John 2*

As mentioned in Chapter 4 of this book, all of God's financial blessings are conditional. You must first do your part, and then God does His part. Victory comes through obedience. Obtaining success in any area of your life requires that you obey God's instructions. God wants to bless you financially, but you must first follow His directives.

> *Observe to do therefore as the Lord your God hath commanded you: ye shall not turn aside to the right hand or to the left. Ye shall walk in all the ways which the Lord your God hath commanded you, that ye may live, and that it may be well with you, and that ye may prolong your days in the land which ye shall possess. Deuteronomy 5:32-33*

You show that you intend to do as you please when you justify why you manage our finances according to your philosophies and make excuses for disobeying God's principles. God is exhorting you to clean up your financial houses and get things in order. In return, He has blessings waiting for you. Nonetheless, because of the stiffed-necked nature, fleshy desires, and stubborn hearts of some individuals, they continue to live beneath their privileges. God wants to restore you!

God promises to make things right. He promises to bless you and restore the bad financial years you endured.

> *And I will restore to you the years that the locust hath eaten, the cankerworm, and the caterpillar, and the palmerworm, my great army which I sent among you. And ye shall eat in plenty, and be satisfied, and praise the name of the LORD your God, that*

hath dealt wondrously with you: and my people shall never be ashamed. Joel 2:25

For many of you, the FOURFOLD PESTS of Joel 2:25 have eaten up:

- Your FINANCES
- Your CONFIDENCE
- Your HOPES and much more

God promises to reimburse you for your losses. What have you lost?" "Which or how many of the locusts have gnawed away at:

- Your SECURITY
- Your PEACE
- Your SENSE OF FULLNESS OF LIFE

God will make a way where there seems to be no way. God will restore you and repay you for your past financial losses. What a challenging and hopeful thought! Removal of shame (Joel 2:26). Once you are restored and your past is repaid, your shame will be removed forever, and you will praise the name of the Lord.

Feelings of shame and guilt usually accompany financial loss. When you lose financially, you feel as if life has lost its vitality. Some of you blame others outwardly, while some of you internalize your pain and secretly blame yourselves. Restoration may remove the external signs of loss by allowing you, as the text says, to "eat in plenty and be satisfied." Praise be to God! According to Scripture, the people of God will never, never, never again be put to shame! Feelings of shame, embarrassment, and inadequacy will be removed forever. Praise God!

What a wonderful promise in exchange for the application of biblical financial principles to our daily lives! "For all the promises of God in Him are yes, and in Him Amen." (2 Corinthians 1:20)

Perhaps you may have endured financial hardships. God wants to restore you.

For your shame ye shall have double; and for confusion they shall

> *rejoice in their portion: therefore, in their land they shall possess the double: everlasting joy shall be unto them. Isaiah 61:7*

The time to reset your financial buttons and prophesy life over your finances is NOW! Many of God's children have strayed from obeying His principles and, as a result, have been slain financially. It is time to let the dry bones in Ezekiel 37:4–7 represent the mortality, transition, and resurrection of your finances and speak life over your finances. You must agree and confess that all your financial needs are met, by God, according to His riches in glory, by Christ Jesus (Philippians 4:19).

God is calling you to a place of restoration.

> *Even from the days of your fathers ye are gone away from Mine ordinances and have not kept them. Return to Me, and I will return unto you; saith the Lord of host. Malachi 3:7*

Perhaps you have gone astray and are not living in accordance with God's financial principles. He commands you to follow His rules. He wants to get you back on track.

> *Ye shall observe to do therefore as The Lord your God hath commanded You: ye shall not turn aside to the right hand or to the left. Ye shall walk in all the ways which the Lord your God hath commanded you, that ye may live, and that it may be well with you, and that ye may prolong your days in the land which ye shall possess.*
> *Deuteronomy 5:32–33*

To get back on track and begin the journey to your financial breakthrough, you must pray, meditate on God's Word, and apply His principles to your daily lifestyles. When you make excuses for disobeying His principles, it simply shows that you intend to continue to do as you please. God is exhorting you to clean up your financial houses and get things in order. For some, because of their stiffed-necked nature, rebellious hearts, and fleshy desires, they continue to live beneath their privileges.

Conclusion

According to an article from Kenneth Copeland Ministries, obedience to God's word will cause you to walk closely with Him. As you follow His direction and leading, you will be able to relish the benefits of your relationship with God.[14] Financial breakthroughs are Included in the benefits. However, you MUST obey God's Word and manage the finances He has given you according to His principles. If you are not faithful in the little things, God will not entrust true riches to you. (Luke 16:11)

If you faithfully apply His principles, you will hear Him say: "Well done, thou good and faithful servant: thou hast been faithful over a few things, I will make thee ruler over many things: enter thou into the joy of thy lord." (Matthew 25:21)

When you encounter situations where there seems to be no way out, you must remember that God can make a way where there seems to be no way. (Isaiah 43:19) At that point, all you need to do is obey His principles and let God be God. Having done ALL His Word tells you to do, you stand and see the salvation of the Lord. The book of Isaiah 55:11 says, "...His word will not return void but will accomplish that which He please." God wishes that, above all things, you prosper and be in good health, even as your soul prospers. (3 John 1:2)

No matter how dark and difficult things may be at present, always remember that things can change at any minute. You can experience your breakthrough suddenly, without warning. Be encouraged. Look up with the expectation that God is going to move suddenly in your life. His Word says: "Behold, I will do a new thing; now it shall spring forth; shall ye not know?" (Isaiah 43:19) Nonetheless, sometimes, although you know, that you know,

14 Kenneth Copeland Ministries 1997-2020

that you know, what God says, and although you believe in your heart, yet your breakthrough can be hindered.

Your breakthrough may be delayed for many reasons. To name a few causes:

- You are not ready to receive a breakthrough. You have not defined your purpose, vision, and mission
- You have not learned what God expects of you
- God is developing your desire to act according to His will when you receive your breakthrough
- God has a divine appointment up ahead
- Your faith is being tested
- There is unbelief and doubt in your heart
- Satan hindered you (1 Thessalonians 2:18)

It is time to make a resolution, a firm decision, to press the reset button on your finances immediately! No matter how disciplined you are, there are times when you will need to evaluate or re-evaluate your finances. Following are a few steps to help you perform an assessment:

- Differentiate a need from a want
- Stop ALL unnecessary spending
- Create or revise your budget
- Look for ways to cut expenses (get less expensive cable, bundle services, etc.)
- Stop using credit cards. You may use it to purchase things that are not in your budget
- Set up payment plans for any outstanding bills
- Request refund of late fees
- Look for areas in your life where you can downsize
- Act like a grown-up. Stop feeling guilty after spending.

A Final Thought

Weeping may endure for a night, but joy cometh in the morning. (Psalm 30:5) Your morning is just around the corner. Perhaps you often prayed about your situation, are in a holding pattern waiting for the answer, and in dire need of a financial breakthrough. God knows all about your financial situation and stands ready to help. He wants to touch your finances and perform a breakthrough miracle in your life. Today could be your appointed time to break through your walls of financial barrier and burst forth into financial freedom!

As you continue to prayerfully align your financial house according to God's financial principles, there is hope! There is a way to escape from all the financial mess. Jesus Christ is the way, the truth, and the life. He invites you to stop fumbling in financial darkness, come back to the love you once knew, and place your trust in Him.

You may have strayed away from God's ordinances. You may have failed to obey His Word and may not have kept His principles. He beckons you to return unto Him, and He will return unto you.

God promises to restore the years that the locust hath eaten—the years that have been devoured up by the various financial crises that have invaded your life. He also promises that His children will never be ashamed. This does not mean that you will be free from financial attacks. Financial challenges will come, but if you manage your affairs according to biblical principles, you will adjust and circumvent the challenges before they become crises. Your financial house will be in order. In return for obedience to the Word of God, you will prosper in every area of your life (including finance) and be in good health, even as your soul prospers. (3 John 1:2) God promises to give all those who trust in Him new hearts and spirits that they will be able to turn their lives around and live. (Ezekiel 11:19; 36:26) God is not slack concerning His promises. (2 Peter 3:9) He is faithful that promised (Hebrews 10:23; 1 Thessalonians 5:24).

The alarm has been sounded.

The message has been delivered.

Will you embrace God's principles of finance
and obtain your Financial Breakthrough?

www.ingramcontent.com/pod-product-compliance
Lightning Source LLC
LaVergne TN
LVHW050945080826
845145LV00004B/1418

* 9 7 8 0 9 8 9 5 4 4 3 2 0 *